ABCDEFGHIJKLMNO

Quaker SAMPLERS

Dedication

Emilio Peire
1955–2021
and
Diane Andrew
1947–2023

Quaker SAMPLERS

The Ultimate Collection of Traditional and Modern Designs

Lesley Wilkins

SEARCH PRESS

First published in 2025
Search Press Limited
Wellwood, North Farm Road,
Tunbridge Wells, Kent TN2 3DR

Printed in China.

ISBN: 978-1-80092-180-1
ebook ISBN: 978-1-80093-163-3

Suppliers

If you have difficulty in obtaining any of the materials and equipment mentioned in this book, then please visit the Search Press website for details of suppliers:

www.searchpress.com

Bookmarked Hub

Extra copies of the stitch diagrams are also available to download free from the Bookmarked Hub. Search for this book by title or ISBN: the files can be found under 'Book Extras'. Membership of the Bookmarked online community is free:

www.bookmarkedhub.com

You are invited to visit the author's Etsy shop:
www.etsy.com/uk/shop/AntiqueSamplerSt

Conversions

The projects in this book have been made using metric measurements, and are presented as width by height. The imperial equivalents provided have been calculated following standard conversion practices. The imperial measurements are often rounded to the nearest ⅛in for ease of use except in rare circumstances; however, if you need more exact measurements, there are a number of excellent online converters that you can use. Always use either metric or imperial measurements, not a combination of both.

TABLE OF CONTENTS

INTRODUCTION

During the seventeenth and eighteenth centuries, the art of sampler making was, for a young girl's education, a pastime and until the late eighteenth century it was only available for the richest or best in society circles.

Ackworth School

In 1779 sampler making became open to those less privileged when a school in North Yorkshire, UK – Ackworth School – was founded by John Fothergill with the intention of educating Quaker families who were less prosperous. From a first attendance of only 49 boys and girls, the school gradually increased to 310 students.

Both male and female pupils were taught writing and arithmetic by the schoolmaster, and the schoolmistress instructed the girls in reading, sewing, knitting and spinning. The boys also worked on the land and gardens and learnt various trades which would lead to apprenticeships.

The art of sampler making at Ackworth School lasted for 60 years, but came to an end without formal explanation by the 1840s. The style and design of the patterns which the pupils embroidered is a mystery to this day and their origin is still unknown. It is thought that the medallions themselves were used for teaching practical geometry – whole, halves and quarters. According to the school's lesson plan, students were given a piece of linen and asked to calculate how to fill the space with full, half and quarter medallions. The resulting elaborate octagonal motifs are today easily identified by sampler enthusiasts as Quaker. Apart from solving mathematical problems, there is no practical use for the medallions and no linens or costume embellishments have ever been discovered.

No evidence has been found to suspect the appointment of a new teacher who may have introduced the medallion patterns. It is unclear why Quakers, who followed plainness and simplicity in clothing and household items, worked such decorative patterns, many of which were stitched in colourful threads.

It has been noted that there was a similarity to German and Northern European medallion motifs used on samplers, but Ackworth samplers, which were dated earlier, were clearly produced first.

Westtown School

In the USA, Westtown School in Chester County, Pennsylvania, was opened in 1799 by the Philadelphia Yearly Meeting to provide Quaker children with a useful education in an environment dedicated to their spiritual formation.

It was in Westtown that girls made samplers and other works of needlecraft. Much of the school was modelled on Ackworth School. Close to Ackworth was York Friends' Girls' School, founded by Esther Tuke in 1785, which also influenced Westtown needlework.

Philadelphia Quakers kept close ties with their ancestral homeland, and some travelled throughout Great Britain as ministers. Their samplers show strong ties between both sides of the Atlantic and the needlework that Westtown produced all derived from styles taught in England. Westtown's first sewing teacher was Elizabeth Bellerby, who had been a student at York Friends' Girls' School in England, so she passed on the styles to her own classes in America.

Sewing was an important part of the eighteenth-century curriculum for English schoolgirls, allowing them to earn a living once they had left, being employed as governesses, teachers or ladies' maids where the ability to do fine sewing was essential. The samplers produced by the girls of Ackworth, Westtown and other Friends schools in England, America and Europe developed a very distinctive individual style during the short time they were produced, and their beauty and mystery continue to fascinate enthusiasts to this day.

Here is a modern sampler showing an octagonal motif and the half medallions we associate with the embroideries produced at Ackworth School and Westtown School.

TOOLS and MATERIALS

Fabric

Quaker design requires an evenweave fabric. Usually, the fabric found in good needlework stores will state the number of holes or threads to the square centimetre or inch. The fewer holes to the square centimetre, the larger a piece of embroidery will be. It is advisable not to choose a very fine fabric for your first project, as it can be very hard on your eyes, and if you are a beginner, counting the threads accurately for a first attempt may prove a little disheartening.

Aida (blockweave)

This is available in various counts and in numerous colours. It is a cotton or cotton mixture fabric which is made especially for counted needlework, with two threads woven into blocks rather than single threads. The majority of my embroideries are worked on this fabric as it gives crisp, accurate results, especially with intricate designs. I have used aida 16 and 18 count (ct) fabric in various shades.

Evenweave

This is a plain, single weave fabric. The number of threads for the warp and the weft are the same, and because the texture is open, the threads are easily counted. Cambric, white and coloured linens are popular evenweave fabrics.

16ct aida, 18ct aida and evenweave fabrics. Most of my embroideries are worked on aida, as it is ideal for intricate designs.

Frames

There are various sizes and types to choose from, depending on the size of your work. Some are available with floor or table stands, clip-on lamps and magnifiers. If you require a magnifier and a lamp attachment, then a floor stand frame would be more beneficial. Thankfully, the days of having a frame in one hand, needle and thread in the other, the chart on your knee, a magnifying glass hung around your neck and the lamp balanced dangerously on the edge of the table are over!

Whichever type of frame you choose, the important rule is to keep your fabric drum-tight.

Embroidery hoops

It is best to use hoops only when the whole of the design fits inside the ring. Moving the hoop around your work can distort the stitches and mark some types of fabric.

Place the fabric over the smaller hoop. Then force the larger hoop over it, making sure that the larger hoop is screwed fairly tightly and the fabric is taut. You will need a screwdriver to loosen the outer hoop and release the fabric.

Rectangular frames

This type of frame, which is available in many sizes, can accommodate the whole width of the fabric, keeping it taut at all times. You do not need a screwdriver to release and move the fabric while you are embroidering – you just move the rollers until you reach the area you want to work on.

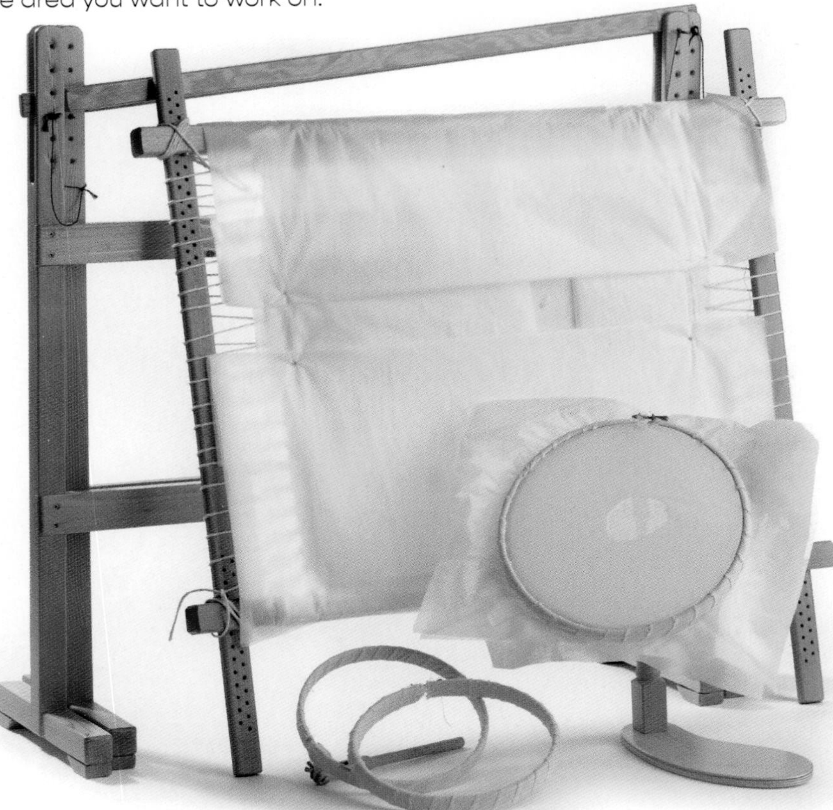

A variety of frames are available, from hand-held hoops to freestanding rectangular frames.

Threads

Today, there is a great variety of threads available for all kinds of embroidery. The choice of threads and their thickness is of course a personal preference and depends on the type of design you are trying to achieve. It is advisable to use short lengths in the needle to avoid knotting. I use DMC stranded cotton because it is available in most craft shop suppliers and online, and is good-quality thread which adds to the appearance of your project.

Organizing your threads

There are many excellent organizing systems you can buy, but I make my own cards by taking a piece of stiff card and punching holes down the side. I cut my skeins into manageable lengths, then take a length, double it and thread the looped end through one of the holes in the card. I push the cut ends through the loop and pull tight. It is easy to remove one length of thread from the card without disturbing the rest. I write the manufacturer's name and the shade number next to the skein.

Another popular way of organizing threads is with reusable plastic thread bobbins. You wind the embroidery thread onto the bobbin and note the shade number on the bobbin. The bobbins can be stored in a bobbin box which keeps them clean, tidy and easier to choose from for your next project.

Stranded cottons

These consist of six strands of cotton and can be separated into groups to provide different thickness and shades.

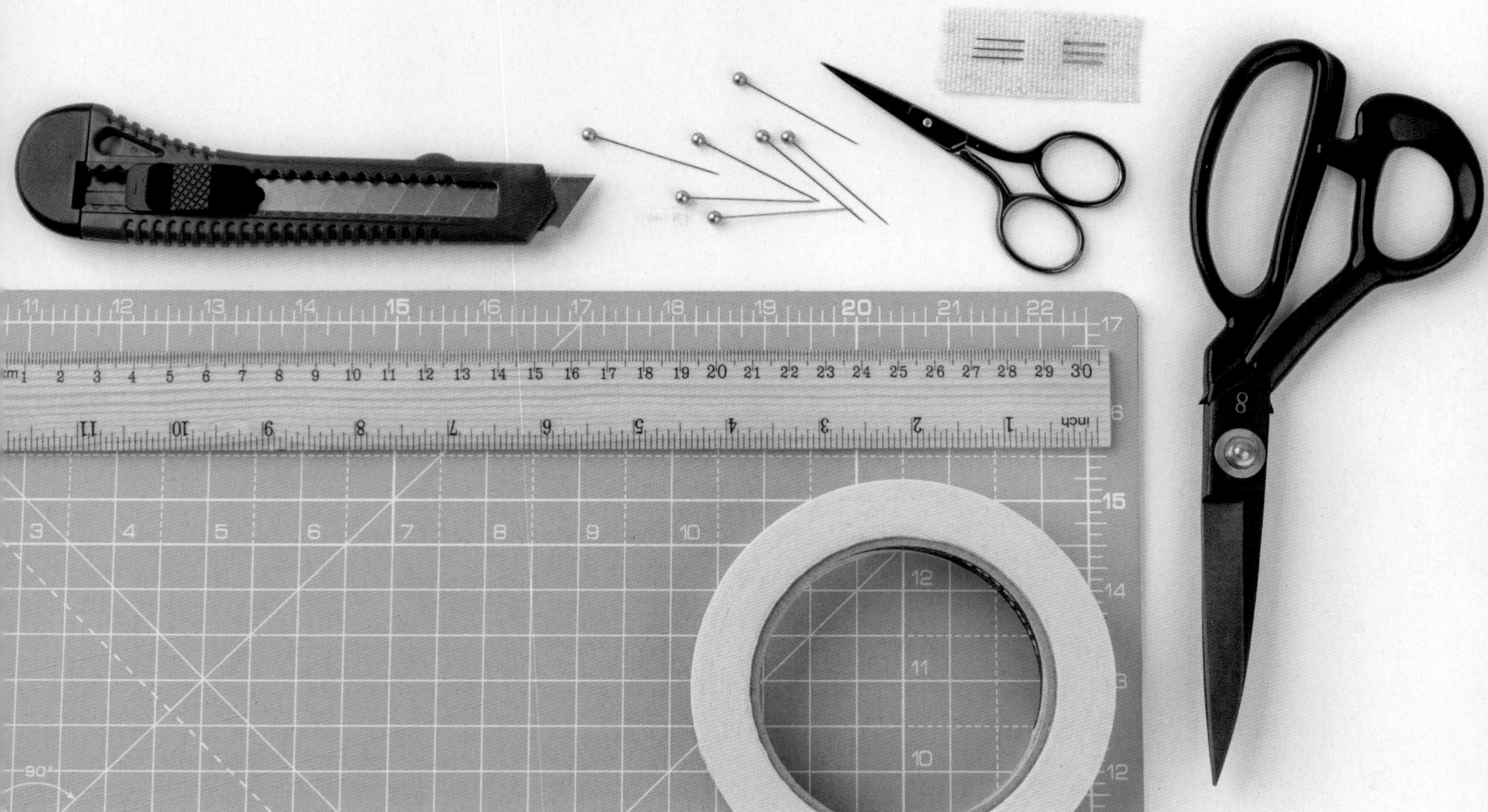

Needles

For all counted needlework you will require a blunt needle. Sharp needles will pierce both the threads on the fabric and the stitches already worked. Also, when the needle passes through the fabric, it should not enlarge or distort the hole – if it does, then it is the wrong size. Finer needles have a larger number and thicker needles a lower number. Sizes 22–26 are usually best. I use a size 24 embroidery needle.

Other items

DRESSMAKER'S SCISSORS
Perfect for cutting out the fabric. Follow the line of the thread when cutting, to make sure you have a straight line.

CUTTING MAT
This is useful when cutting mounting board with a craft knife.

IRON
(not shown) Use an iron to press an embroidery gently on the back before mounting it.

EMBROIDERY SCISSORS
These are useful for unpicking mistakes. They should be kept sharp to prevent them from chewing the thread. The point should be fine enough to slip under the stitch to cut it.

PINS
Use pins to mark the centre of your fabric and hold it in place when you are mounting an embroidery.

RULER OR MEASURING TAPE
Use these to measure when choosing fabric and when mounting embroideries.

MASKING TAPE
Use masking tape to prevent fabric from fraying.

HOLE PUNCH
(not shown) This is useful for making a thread organizer.

CRAFT KNIFE, ACID-FREE MOUNTING BOARD AND DOUBLE-SIDED TAPE
These are used for mounting your finished work.

GETTING STARTED

Workspace

Each person has their own way of working, holding a frame balanced on their lap or supported by a stand, and sitting on a stool or in a comfortable armchair.

I have a special work box close to hand containing everything I need for a particular project, and I support my frame with a seat frame holder. This enables me to sit comfortably with the frame in my lap, and work freely with both hands. The most important thing to consider is comfort and good back support while you work, and having your materials close by.

Natural daylight is best for embroidery, so sit near a window for the best results. If you have to sew at night, work under a good lamp which should be positioned on the left if you are right-handed, or on the right if you are left-handed, to prevent working in your own shadow. Daylight bulbs, although expensive, are worth investing in and give an excellent clear, natural light.

Outdoor sewing can lead to all sorts of disasters, such as dropping the work on the ground or insects getting squashed on the fabric.

Using charts

The most important part of the chart is the point at which you will place your first stitch. Quaker designs can be very intricate, so the centre point of the chart and fabric is where you should begin. If you start in the wrong place, you may find halfway through your work that you have run out of space, and hours of work will be wasted.

When you have cut your fabric using the sizes given in the instructions, make sure you also leave at least 5cm (2in) extra all the way round. To find the centre of the fabric, fold it in half once, lightly pressing a crease mark on the centre fold, then fold the fabric in half again. This will leave a cross mark. Place a pin on this centre point and open out the fabric. The pin will be dead centre in the fabric and your starting marker.

To find the centre of the chart, check the stitch count on the instructions, e.g. 105 x 112. Count 52 squares across which is the nearest square to the top centre of the chart, then from this marker count downwards 56 squares. Mark this square, which is the centre of the chart and where you will begin. Always go to the nearest square if it's an odd not even count.

Once the centre motif has been completed, work the surrounding patterns in any order until you reach the outer edges.

Most of the designs in this book appear in chart form, to show the patterns clearly and to enable you to design your own samplers.

Basic stitches

I use two basic stitches in my designs. Cross stitch is the main stitch I use, and this is indicated by squares on the charts. Some of my designs also use back stitch, and this is shown as vertical, horizontal or diagonal lines within the squares on the charts.

Cross stitch

This is a very simple stitch, but it can look untidy if the directions of the top stitches differ, so always make sure they face in the same direction.

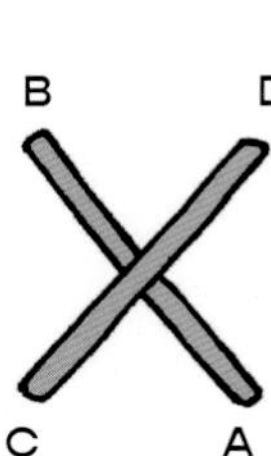

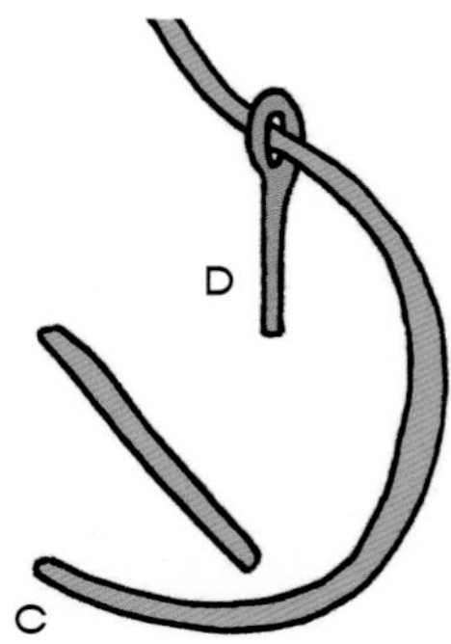

1. Start at point A. Take the needle diagonally to the left and insert it at B.

2. Bring the needle up at point C and insert down at D. For the next stitch, bring the needle up at point C (which then becomes A) and repeat the procedure.

Back stitch

Back stitch is used as the basis for many other stitches, and can be used as an outline stitch.

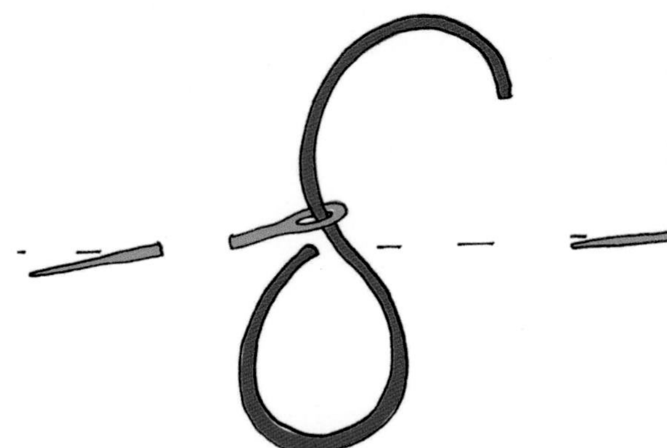

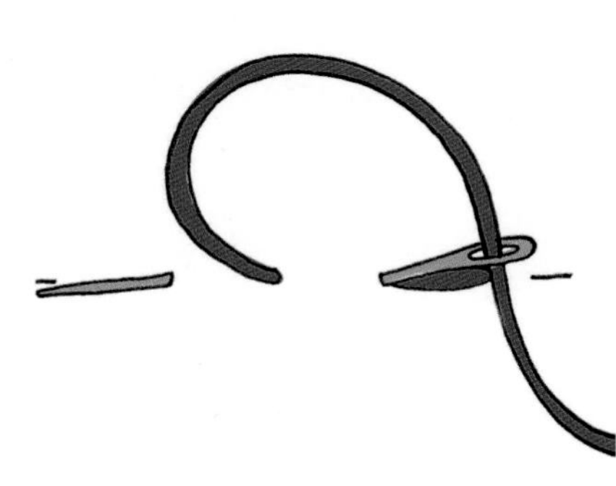

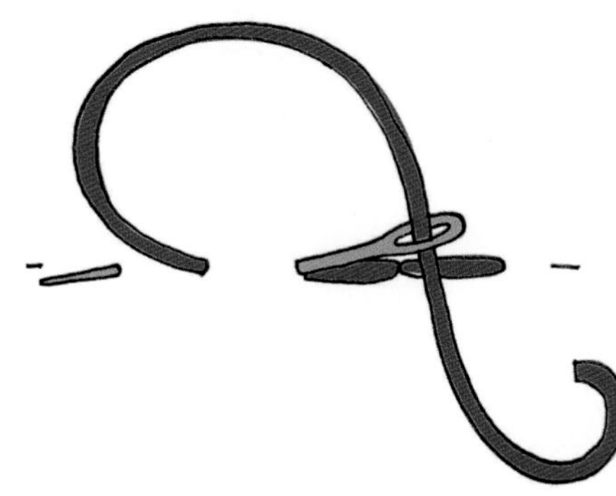

1. Bring the needle up to the right side of the material. Take it back along the line and go down to the wrong side. Bring the needle up to the right side again, in front of the first stitch, a stitch length away.

2. Always finish the stitch by inserting the needle at the point where the last stitch began.

3. Repeat.

TRADITIONAL QUAKER DESIGNS

There is something quite mysterious about Quaker samplers: who first created all of these different patterns, medallions and motifs, which for 60 years were worked by the pupils in the Quaker schools in England and America? To this day it remains an unanswered question, and in a way it adds to the samplers' charm and beauty.

The traditional designs that follow are in keeping with the many original samplers found in the Ackworth School collection and American schools such as Westtown, which all followed the same patterns and similar layouts.

L W

ABCDEFGHIJKLMN
OPQRSTUVWXYZ
2022

ABCDEFGHIJKLMNO
PQRSTUVWXYZ
ABCDEFGHIJKLMNOPQRSTUVWX
YZ abcdefghijklmnopqrstuvwxyz

2022

SAMPLER 1

Design size

112 x 108 stitch count

17.5 x 16cm (7 x 6¼in)

Materials

Fabric

16ct aida Oatmeal Rustico, Zweigart

Using alternative fabric may affect the finished size

DMC stranded cotton

3 skeins of blue mix 4025

Use 2 strands of thread throughout

Tapestry needle

Size 24

Construction diagram

This is a small sampler and is quick and easy to work, with only one chart to follow.

See chart on page 36.

SAMPLER 2

Design size

97 x 105 stitch count

13.75 x 14.5cm (5½ x 5¾in)

Materials

Fabric

18ct aida Oatmeal Rustico, Zweigart

Using alternative fabric may affect the finished size

DMC stranded cotton

1 skein of brown 3860

Use 2 strands of thread throughout

Tapestry needle

Size 24

Construction diagram

This is a small sampler and is quick and easy to work, with only one chart to follow.

See chart on page 37.

2022

SAMPLER 3

Design size

105 x 112 stitch count

14.5 x 16cm (5½ x 6¼in)

Materials

Fabric

18ct aida Oatmeal Rustico, Zweigart

Using alternative fabric may affect the finished size

DMC stranded cotton

2 skeins of dark green 520

1 skein of light green 989

Use 2 strands of thread throughout

Tapestry needle

Size 24

Construction diagram

This is a small sampler and is quick and easy to work.

See charts on pages 38–39.

SAMPLER 4

Design size

279 x 237 stitch count

38 x 33cm (15 x 13in)

Materials

Fabric

18ct aida Oatmeal Rustico, Zweigart

Using alternative fabric may affect the finished size

DMC stranded cotton

7 skeins of black 310

1 skein of pink 316

Use 2 strands of thread throughout

Tapestry needle

Size 24

Construction diagram

Work this sampler piecing the charts together as shown. See charts on pages 40–45.

Using the alphabet chart on page 39, you can swap the letters I have chosen to embroider with your own, meaningful, initials to personalize your work.

SAMPLER 5

Design size

230 x 143 stitch count

37 x 22cm (14½ x 8¾in)

Materials

Fabric

16ct aida Antique White, Zweigart

Using alternative fabric may affect the finished size

DMC stranded cotton

3 skeins of black 310

2 skeins of peach 407

Use 2 strands of thread throughout

Tapestry needle

Size 24

Construction diagram

Work this sampler piecing the charts together as shown.
See charts on pages 46–48.

A

B

C

D

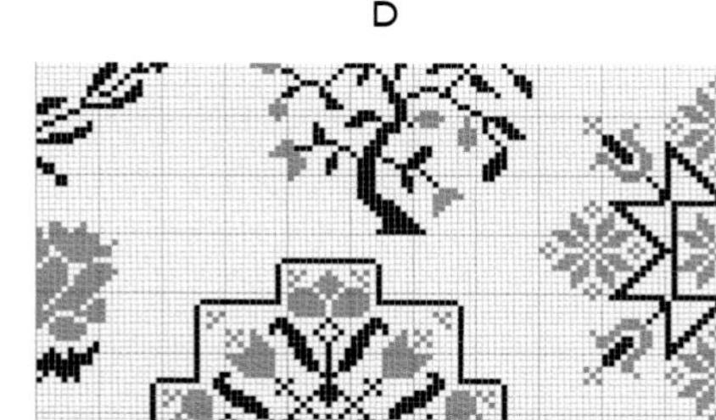

You can personalize the centre motif with your choice of initials, as on Sampler 3, page 21, which uses the same initial graph.

SAMPLER 6

Design size

180 x 250 stitch count

26.5 x 36cm (10½ x 14in)

Materials

Fabric

18ct aida Antique White, Zweigart

Using alternative fabric may affect the finished size

DMC stranded cotton

5 skeins of grey 3768

Use 2 strands of thread throughout

Tapestry needle

Size 24

Construction diagram

Work this sampler piecing the charts together as shown.
See charts on pages 49–51.

A

B

C

SAMPLER 7

Design size

79 x 230 stitch count

12.5 x 35.5cm (5 x 14in)

Materials

Fabric

16ct aida Antique White, Zweigart

Using alternative fabric may affect the finished size

DMC stranded cotton

3 skeins of purple 3740

Use 2 strands of thread throughout

Tapestry needle

Size 24

Construction diagram

Work this sampler piecing the charts together as shown.

See charts on pages 52–53.

A

B

SAMPLER 8

Design size

186 x 84 stitch count

27.5 x 12cm (10¾ x 4¾in)

Construction diagram

Work this sampler piecing the charts together as shown.

See charts on pages 54–55.

A

B

Materials

Fabric

18ct aida Antique White, Zweigart

Using alternative fabric may affect the finished size

DMC stranded cotton

1 skein of dark brown 3790

1 skein of light brown 841

1 skein of dark green 501

1 skein of medium green 503

1 skein of dark grey 317

1 skein of light grey 318

Use 2 strands of thread throughout

Tapestry needle

Size 24

TOP

SAMPLER 9

Design size

149 x 312 stitch count

21 x 43.75cm (8¼ x 17¼in)

Materials

Fabric

18ct aida Oatmeal Rustico, Zweigart

Using alternative fabric may affect the finished size

DMC stranded cotton

5 skeins of black 310

Use 2 strands of thread throughout

Tapestry needle

Size 24

Construction diagram

Work this sampler piecing the charts together as shown.

See charts on pages 56–58.

A

B

C

A
token
of love

SAMPLER 10

Design size

157 x 304 stitch count

22.25 x 42cm (8¾ x 16½in)

Materials

Fabric

18ct aida Oatmeal Rustico, Zweigart

Using alternative fabric may affect the finished size

DMC stranded cotton

1 skein of dark brown 840

1 skein of yellow 676

1 skein of dark blue 930

1 skein of medium blue 932

1 skein of light blue/green 927

1 skein of medium peach 758

1 skein of dark green 520

1 skein of light green 3052

1 skein of dark pink 3722

1 skein of light pink 224

1 skein of mauve 3042

Use 2 strands of thread throughout

Tapestry needle

Size 24

Construction diagram

Work this sampler piecing the charts together as shown.

See charts on pages 59–61.

A

B

C

ABCDEFGHIJKLMN
OPQRSTUVWXYZ
L W
2022

TRADITIONAL CHARTS

Key

- Cross stitch
- Back stitch

Sampler 1 See pages 16–17

Sampler 2 See pages 18–19

Sampler 3 See pages 20–21

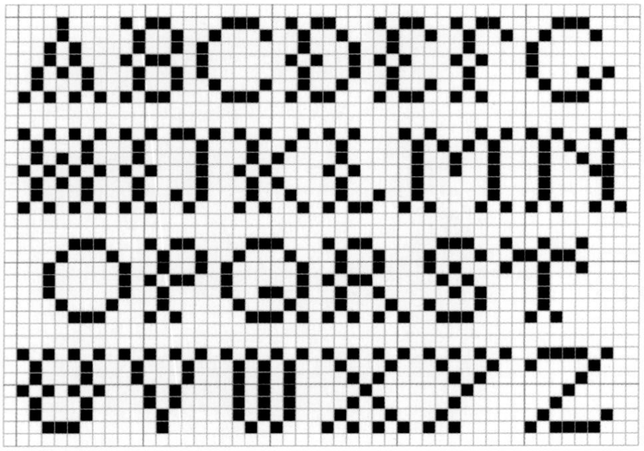

Sampler 4 See pages 22–23

Using the alphabet chart on page 39, you can swap the letters I have chosen to embroider with your own, meaningful, initials to personalize your work.

B

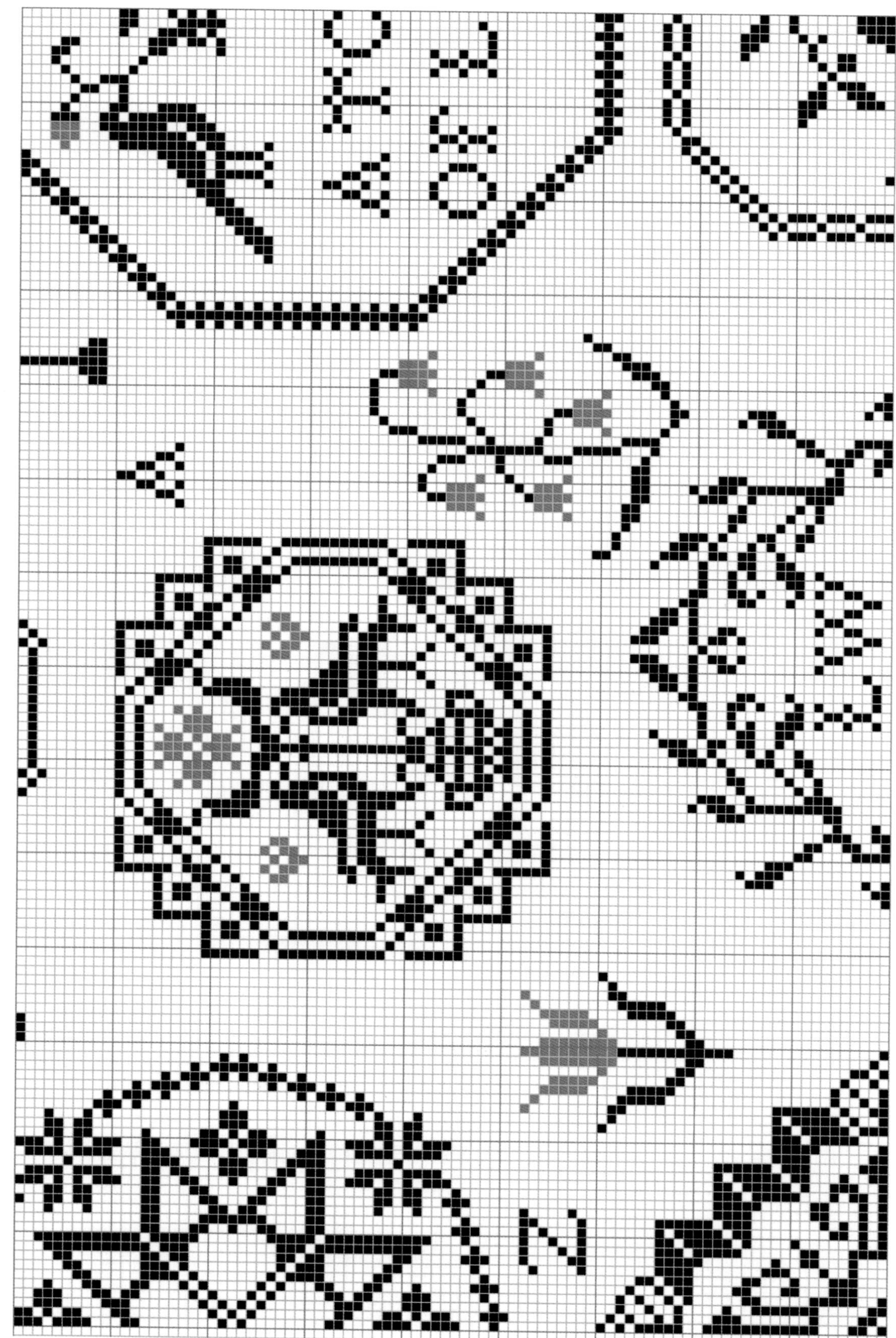

D

E

F

Sampler 5 See pages 24–25

A

You can personalize the centre motif with your choice of initials, as on Sampler 3, (see charts on pages 38–39), which uses the same initial graph.

B

C

D

Sampler 6

See pages 26–27

A

B

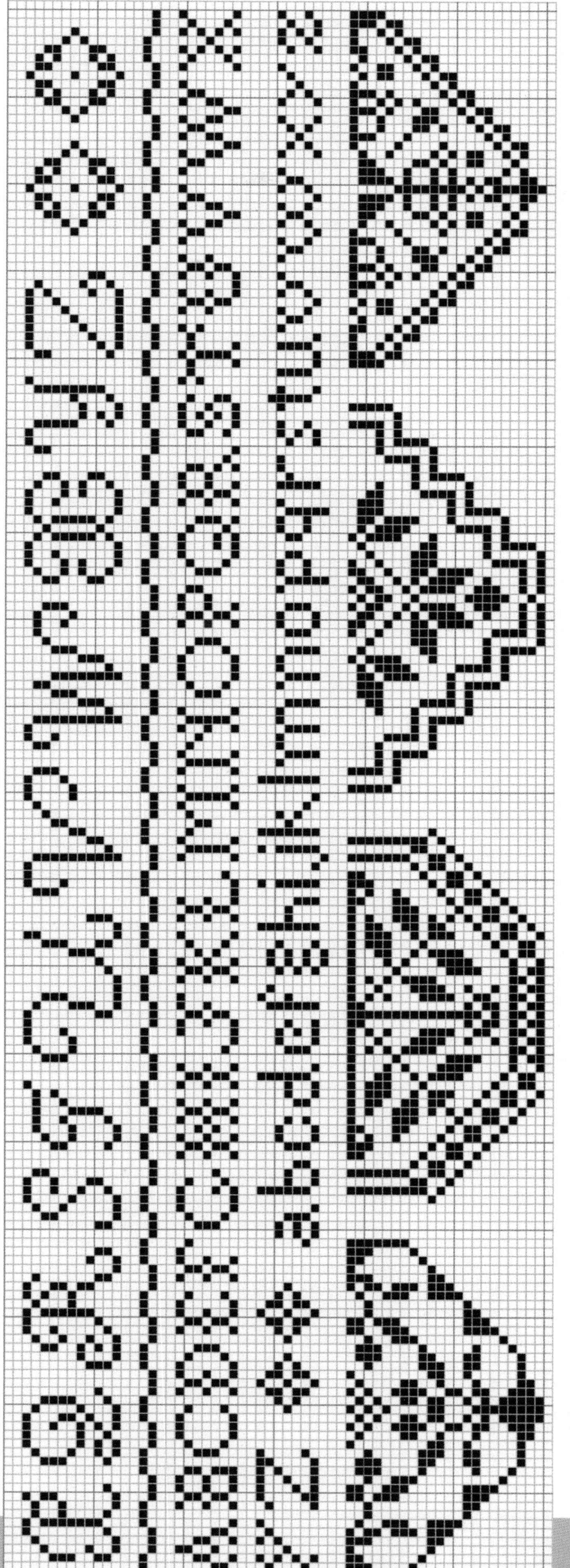

C

Sampler 7 See pages 28–29

A

B

Sampler 8 See pages 30–31

A

B

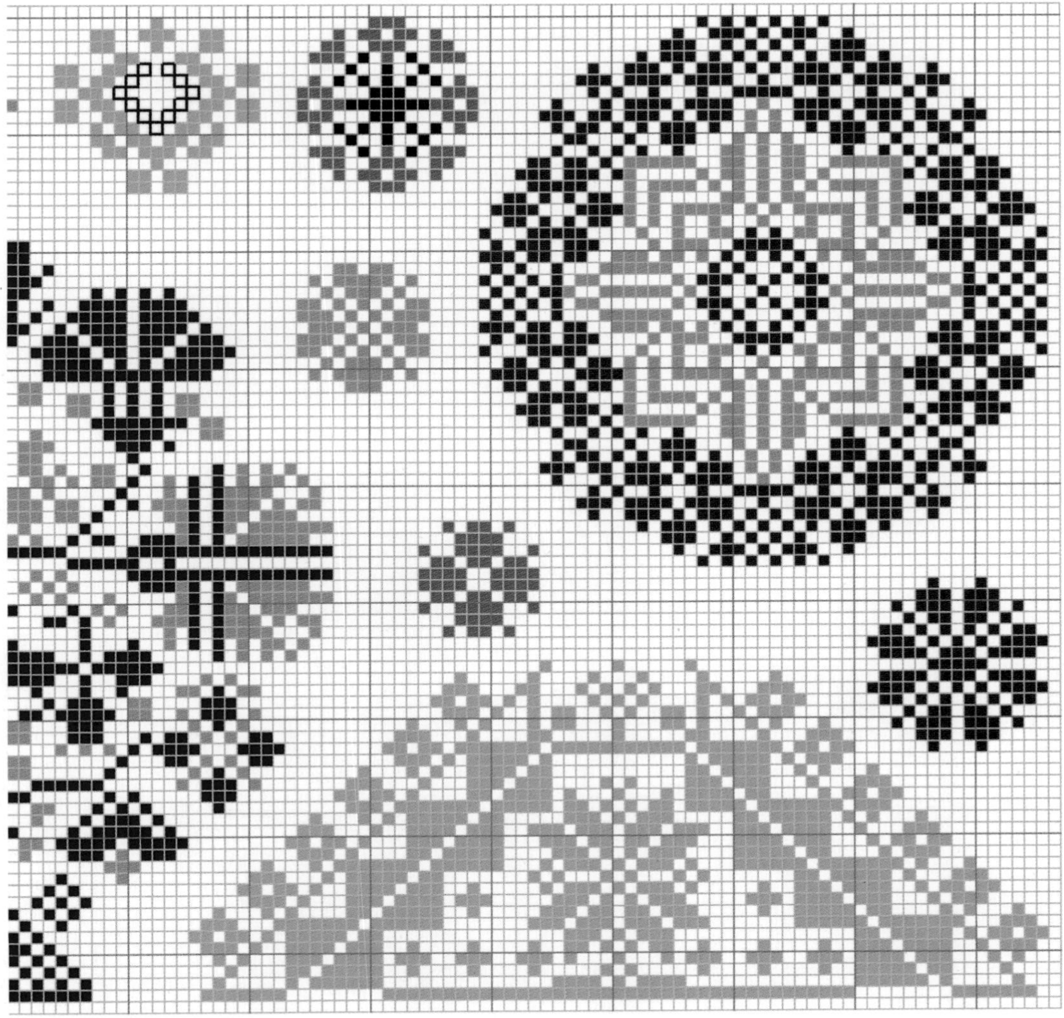

Sampler 9 See pages 32–33

A

B

C

 See pages 34–35

B

C

You can swap the letters and date I have chosen to embroider with your own, to personalize your work.

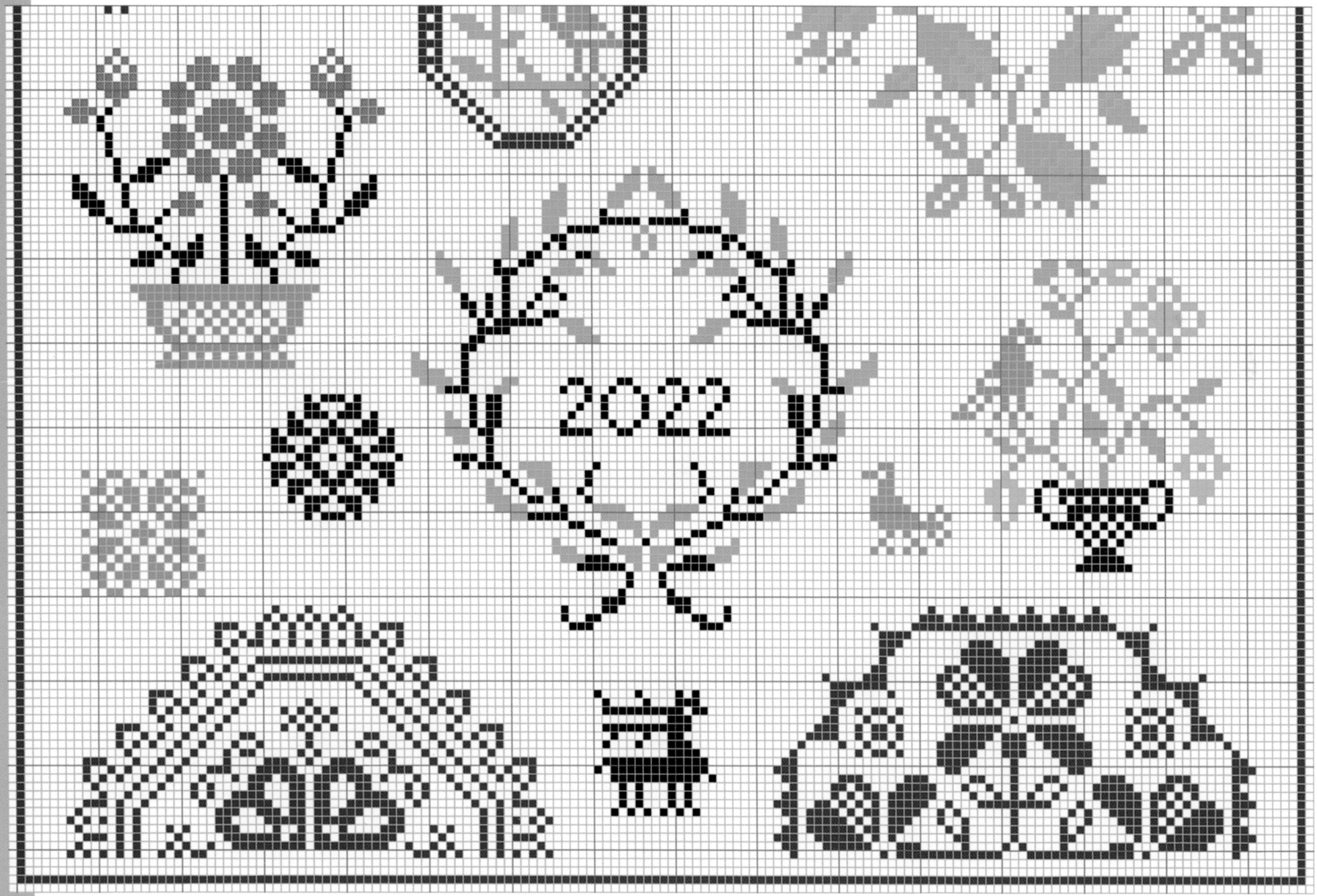

2022

MODERN QUAKER DESIGNS

As with many of the historic samplers which have been worked over the centuries, it is due to the popularity of current designers and embroiderers that the unique patterns have been passed on and will hopefully continue well into the future.

It only takes a little imagination to design your own, and there are many examples in the Stitch Directory on pages 98–119 to help you create your own samplers and special items.

A token of love

ABCD
EFGH
UVW
XYZ

SAMPLER 1

Design size

93 x 85 stitch count

14.25 x 13cm (5½ x 5in)

Materials

Fabric

16ct aida Antique White, Zweigart

Using alternative fabric may affect the finished size

DMC stranded cotton

1 skein of red 815

Use 2 strands of thread throughout

Tapestry needle

Size 24

Construction diagram

This is a small sampler and is quick and easy to work, with only one chart to follow.

See chart on page 84.

SAMPLER 2

Design size

77 x 124 stitch count

9.5 x 15.25cm (3¾ x 6in)

Materials

Fabric

18ct aida Antique White, Zweigart

Using alternative fabric may affect the finished size

DMC stranded cotton

2 skeins of dark green 501

Use 2 strands of thread throughout

Tapestry needle

Size 24

Construction diagram

This is a small sampler and is quick and easy to work, with only one chart to follow.

See chart on page 85.

SAMPLER 3

Design size

122 x 119 stitch count

15.5 x 15cm (6¼ x 6in)

Materials

Fabric

20ct Floba

Using alternative fabric may affect the finished size

DMC stranded cotton

2 skeins of mauve 3041

Use 2 strands of thread throughout

Tapestry needle

Size 24

Construction diagram

This is a small sampler and is quick and easy to work, with only one chart to follow.

See chart on page 86.

SAMPLER 4

Design size

115 x 69 stitch count

18.25 x 10.75cm (7¼ x 4¼in)

Construction diagram

This is a small sampler and is quick and easy to work, with only one chart to follow.

See chart on page 87.

Materials

Fabric

16ct aida Antique White, Zweigart

Using alternative fabric may affect the finished size

DMC stranded cotton

2 skeins of pink 3687

Use 2 strands of thread throughout

Tapestry needle

Size 24

FRIENDS

SAMPLER 5

Design size

139 x 89 stitch count

20 x 12.5cm (7¾ x 5in)

Materials

Fabric

16ct aida Oatmeal Rustico, Zweigart

Using alternative fabric may affect the finished size

DMC stranded cotton

3 skeins of blue mix 4240

Use 2 strands of thread throughout

Tapestry needle

Size 24

Construction diagram

Work this sampler following the chart on page 88.

ABCDEFGHIJKLMNOPQRS
TUVWXYZ abcdefghijklm
nopqrstuvwxyz

SAMPLER 6

Design size

153 x 87 stitch count

21.75 x 12.25cm (8½ x 4¾in)

Construction diagram

Work this sampler following the chart on page 89.

Materials

Fabric

16ct aida Oatmeal Rustico, Zweigart

Using alternative fabric may affect the finished size

DMC stranded cotton

3 skeins of red mix 4210

Use 2 strands of thread throughout

Tapestry needle

Size 24

A token of love

SAMPLER 7

Design size

155 x 139 stitch count

21.75 x 19.25cm (8½ x 7½in)

Materials

Fabric

18ct aida Oatmeal Rustico, Zweigart

Using alternative fabric may affect the finished size

DMC stranded cotton

3 skeins of blue 931

Use 2 strands of thread throughout

Tapestry needle

Size 24

Construction diagram

Work this sampler piecing the charts together as shown. See charts on pages 90–91.

A

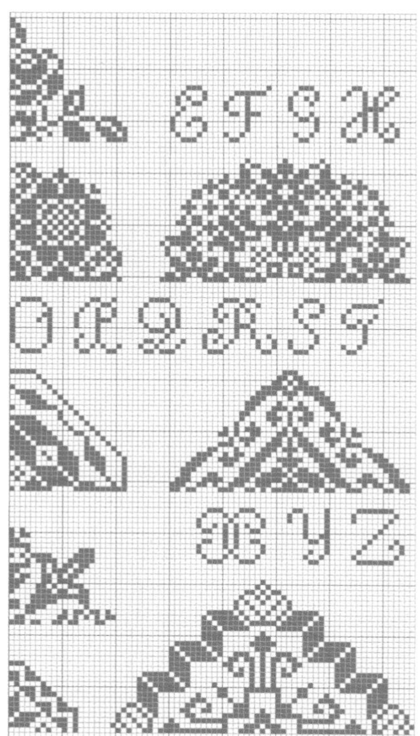

SAMPLER 8

Design size

126 x 133 stitch count

17 x 19cm (6¾ x 7½in)

Materials

Fabric

18ct aida Antique White, Zweigart

Using alternative fabric may affect the finished size

DMC stranded cotton

1 skein of brown 841

1 skein of mauve 3042

1 skein of light blue/green 927

1 skein of yellow 738

1 skein of pink 224

1 skein of blue 932

Use 2 strands of thread throughout

Tapestry needle

Size 24

Construction diagram

Work this sampler piecing the charts together as shown.
See charts on pages 92–93.

A

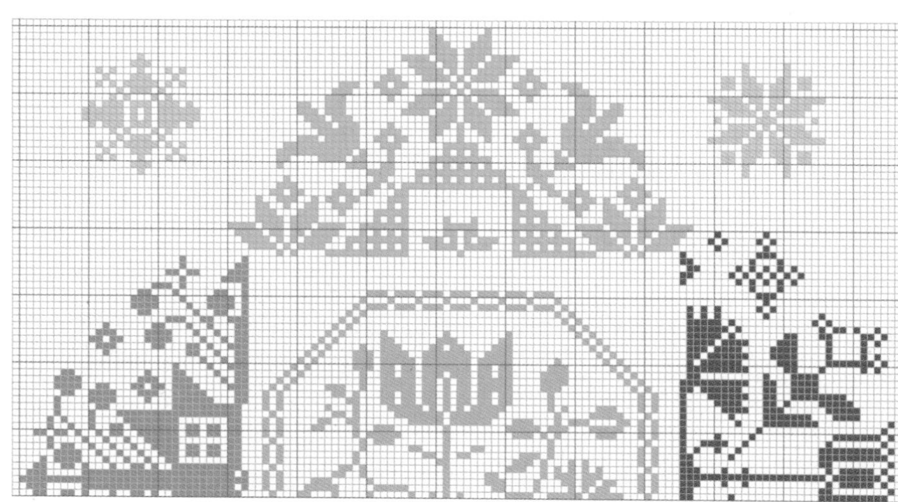

B

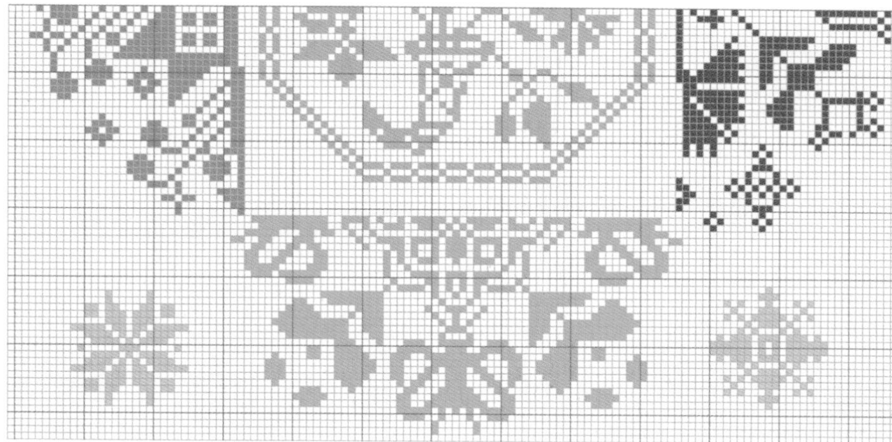

SAMPLER 9

Design size

220 x 71 stitch count

32.5 x 10.25cm (12¾ x 4in)

Materials

Fabric

18ct aida Antique White, Zweigart

Using alternative fabric may affect the finished size

DMC stranded cotton

1 skein of mauve 3041

1 skein of dark green 3051

1 skein of light green 3053

1 skein of yellow 437

1 skein of grey 926

1 skein of blue 932

Use 2 strands of thread throughout

Tapestry needle

Size 24

Construction diagram

Work this sampler piecing the charts together as shown.

See charts on pages 94–95.

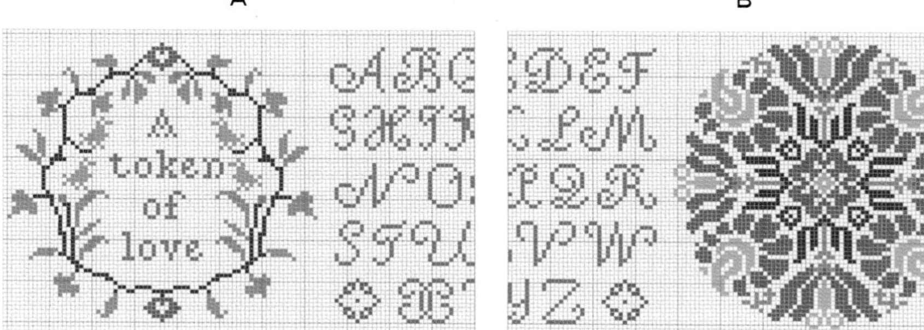

A
token
of
love

ABCDEF
GHIKLM
NOPQR
STUVW
XYZ

SAMPLER 10

Design size

107 x 205 stitch count

17 x 32cm (6¾ x 12½in)

Materials

Fabric

16ct aida Antique White, Zweigart

Using alternative fabric may affect the finished size

DMC stranded cotton

1 skein of dark pink 3721

1 skein of medium pink 223

1 skein of light pink 152

1 skein of dark grey 317

1 skein of light grey 318

Use 2 strands of thread throughout

Tapestry needle

Size 24

Construction diagram

Work this sampler piecing the charts together as shown. See charts on pages 96–97.

A

B

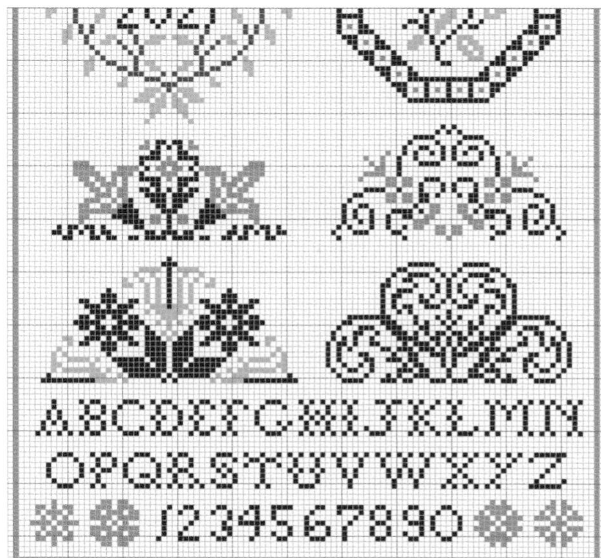

E P
2021
ABCDEFGHIJKLMN
OPQRSTUVWXYZ
1234567890

MODERN CHARTS

Key

- Cross stitch
- Back stitch

Sampler 1 See pages 64–65

Sampler 2 See pages 66–67

Sampler 3 See pages 68–69

Sampler 4 See pages 70–71

Sampler 5 See pages 72–73

Sampler 6

See pages 74–75

Sampler 7 See pages 76–77

A

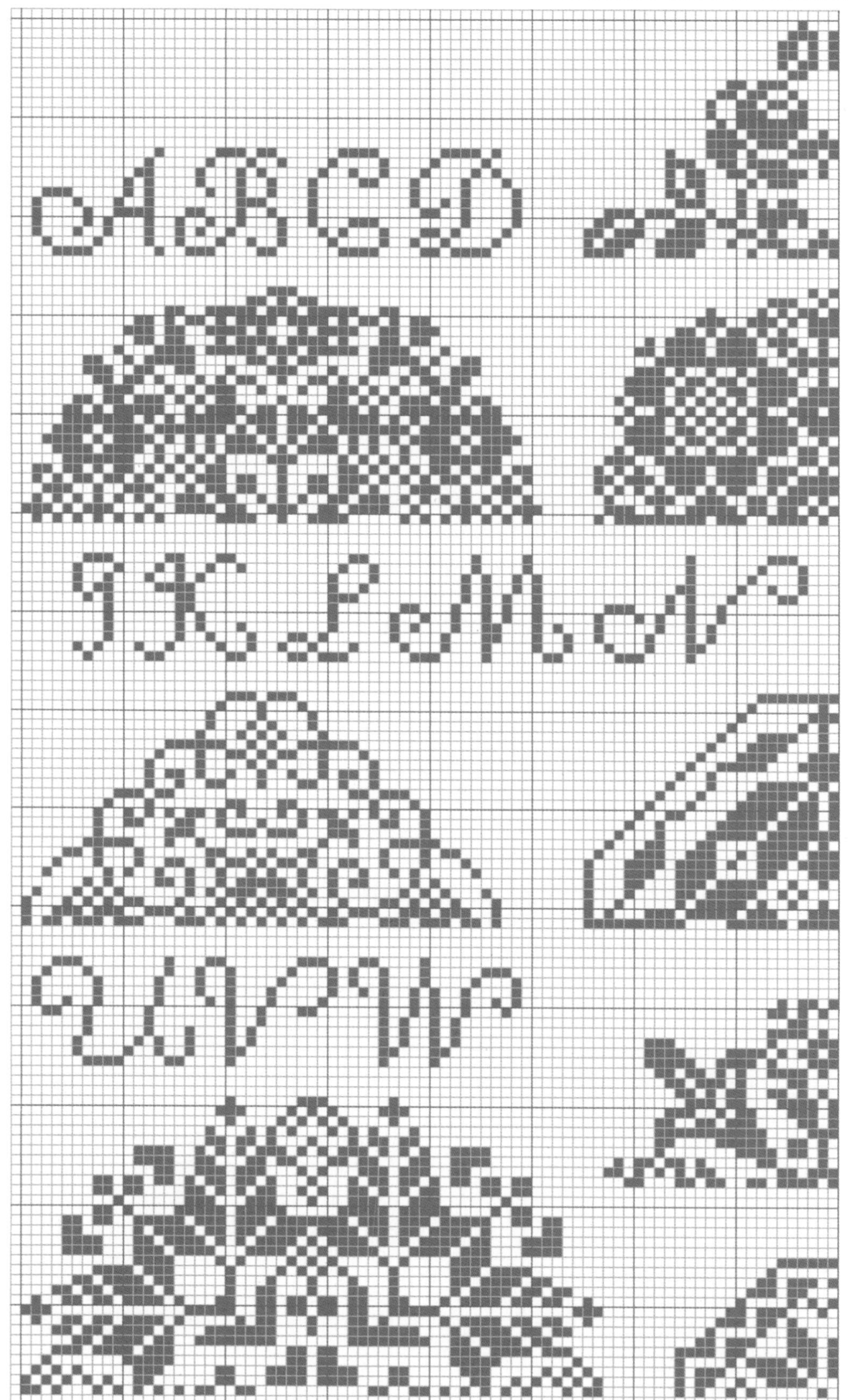

B

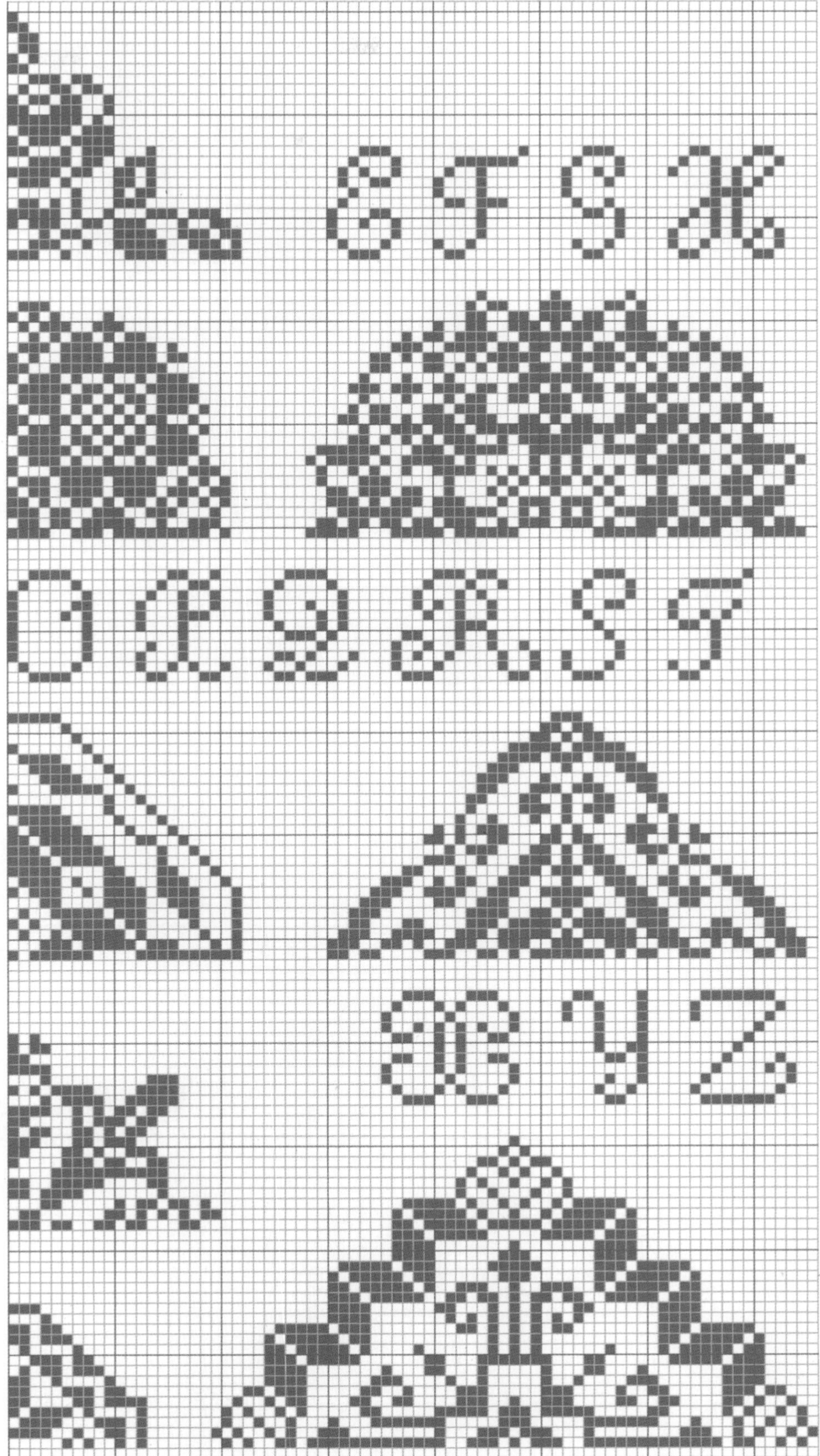

Sampler 8 See pages 78–79

A

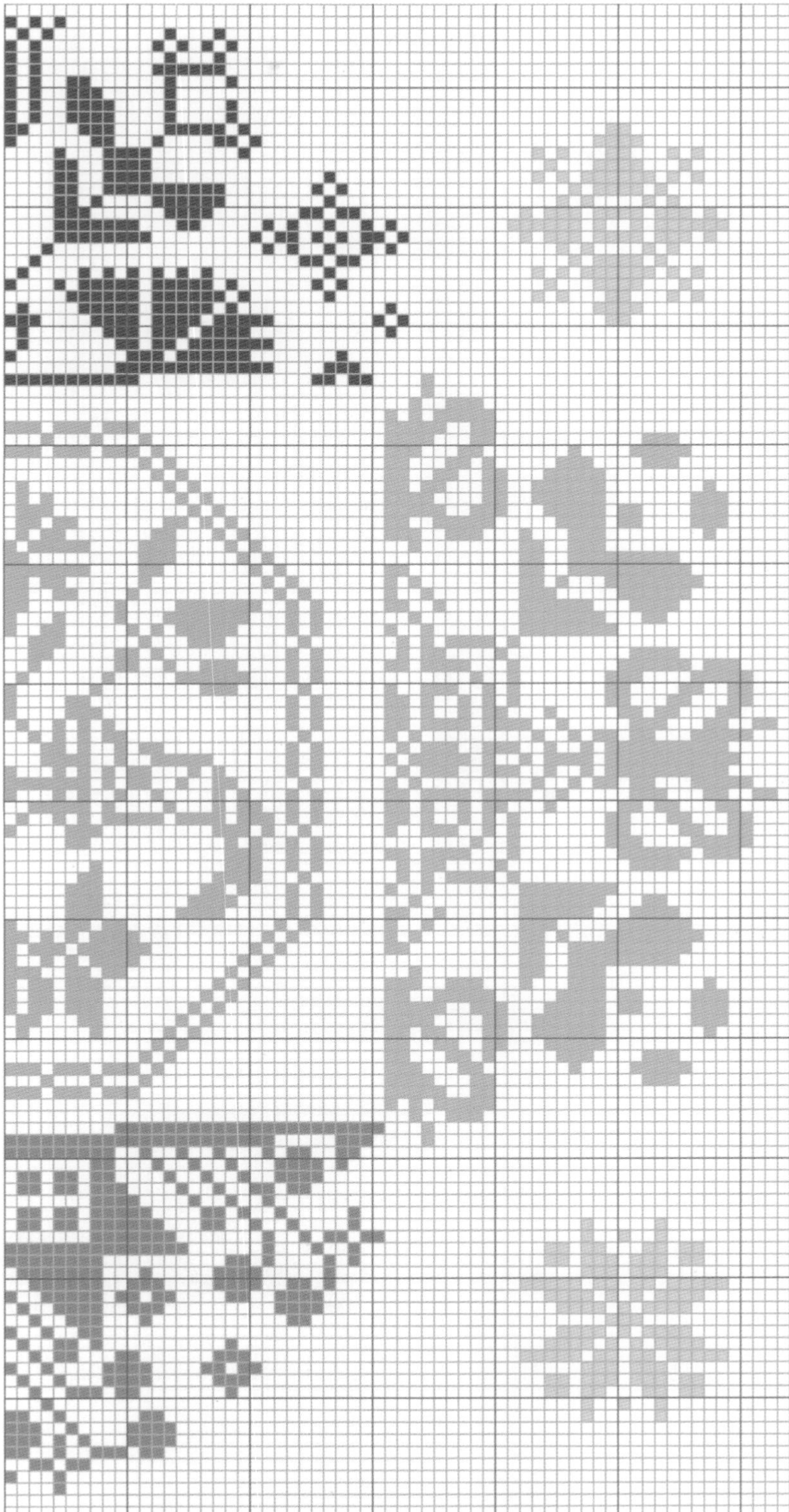

B

Sampler 9 See pages 80–81

A

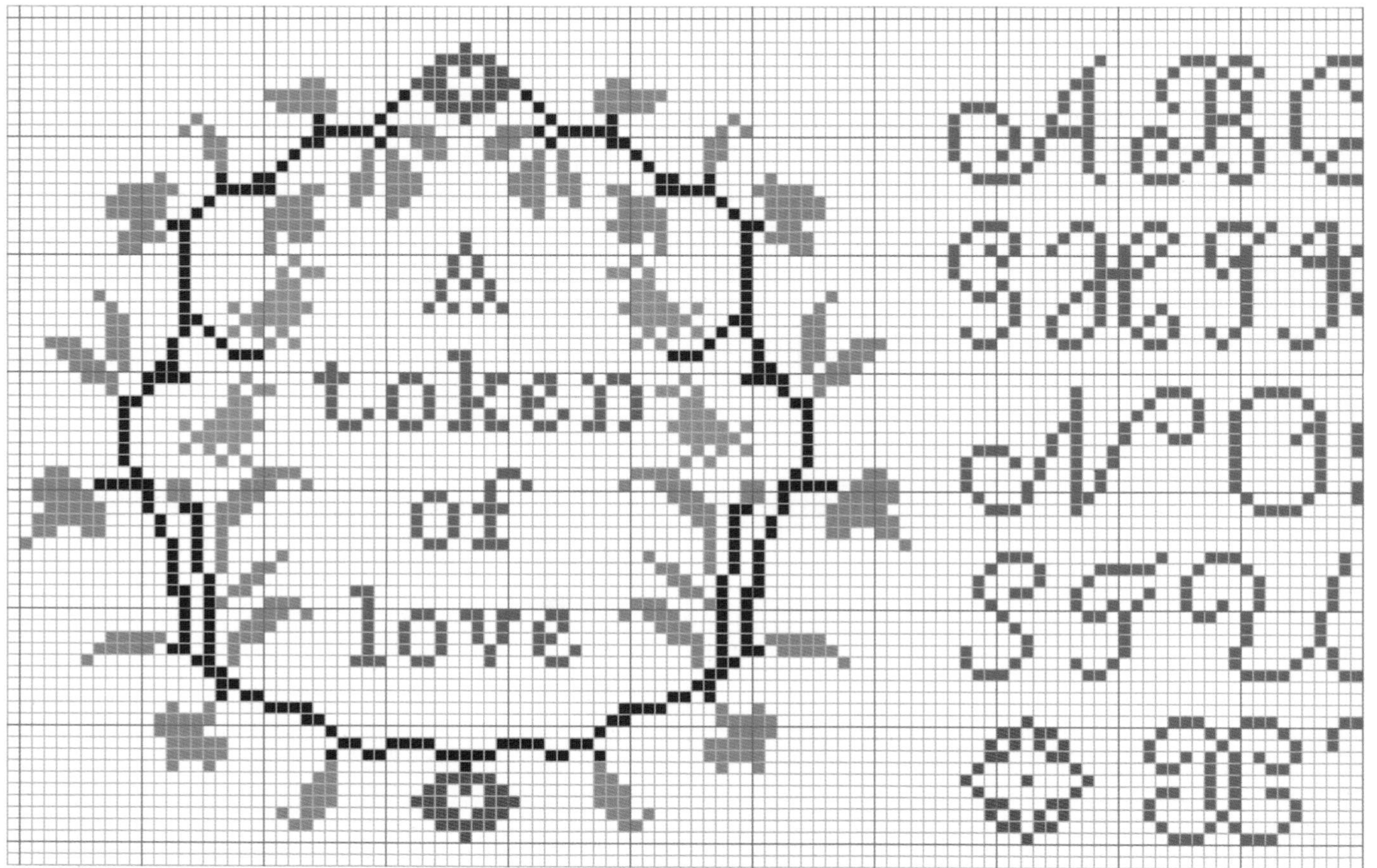

B

Sampler 10 See pages 82–83

A

B

STITCH DIRECTORY

Medallion samplers are the most decorative and ornamental of the embroideries we associate with Ackworth School and Quaker style. By the standards of the day, they were quite simple in their design, but they are as decorative as anything the pupils were allowed to create.

Although this type of sampler is generally referred to as a medallion sampler, it is common to find the following motifs: stylized sprays of flowers, wreaths, paired birds, and initials. These are distinctive to Quaker instruction.

Although a great number of medallion samplers were worked in one colour, colours other than black and brown were used; blue, green and red were not uncommon. There are also many polychrome examples; these are quite lively in comparison to the monochrome embroideries. Even when multiple colours were allowed, the selection was still limited to subdued earthy shades.

Early medallion samplers

The earliest known Ackworth medallion sampler was worked in 1783 by Benjamina Rickman (see below). She was a Quaker girl from Westminster, London, who was a pupil at Ackworth School from 1780 to 1785. Her sampler is very plain and features her name, the school name and the year in which she stitched her sampler.

Another early medallion sampler in the Ackworth collection was worked in 1790 by Mary Wigham (see opposite). Mary lived in Pontefract and attended Ackworth School from 1788 to 1791. Her sampler is a good example of a medallion sampler because it contains all the motifs previously mentioned. Mary worked half medallions to form the border, and

Benjamina Rickman, sampler, 1783, 16 x 9 cm, RSN 2265. © Royal School of Needlework.

included five full medallions in the centre, one with paired birds in the centre. She placed various sprays of flowers, a wreath composed of flowers, and many initials throughout her sampler.

Because it is embroidered in polychrome, it is a fine example of the subdued colours that were acceptable and in compliance with Quaker rules of plainness and simplicity.

There is no apparent practical use of the medallion or other motifs that appear on these samplers and they are completely different to the marking and darning samplers and extracts of religious text and verse worked at Ackworth School. It is not known who decided that the medallions were an appropriate motif for the school to sanction. Neither dress nor linens were embellished with any of these motifs.

This section includes a selection of the most popular motifs the pupils of Ackworth School stitched, which can form the basis of your own samplers, large, small or individual motifs.

Mary Wigham, sampler, 1790.
© Ackworth School Estates Ltd.

Key
Cross stitch
Back stitch

L W

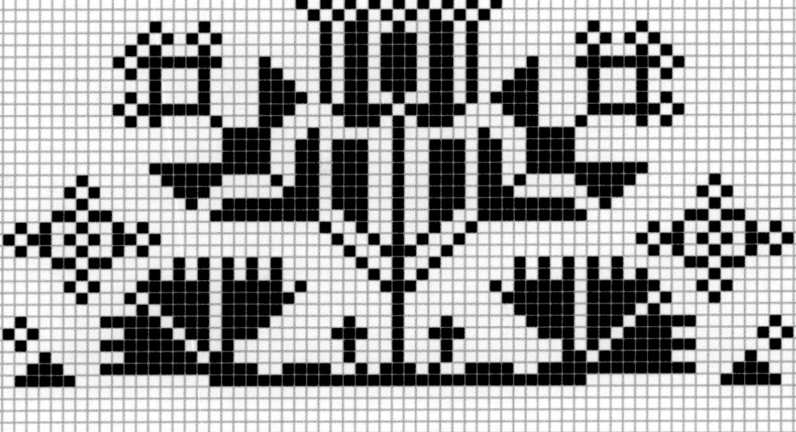

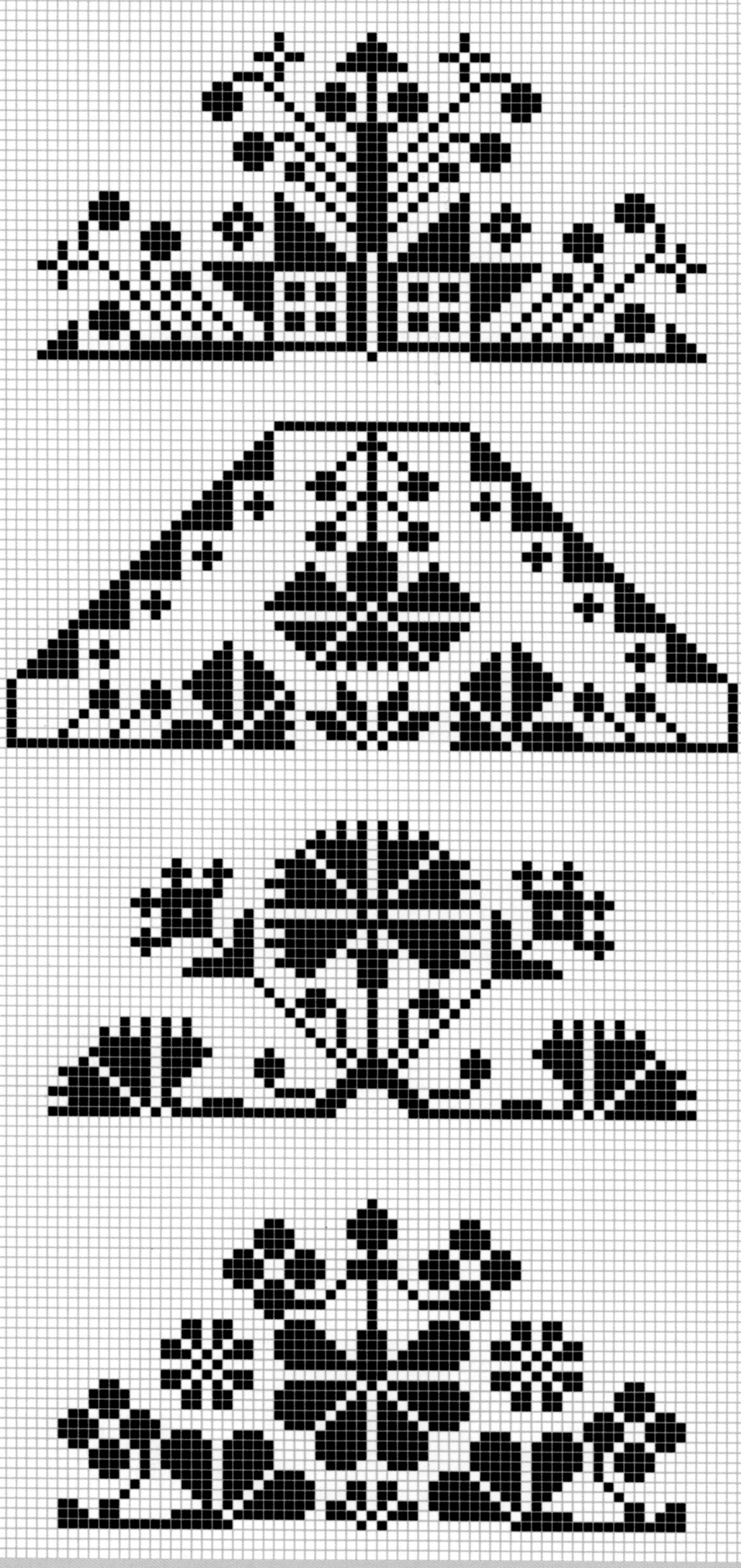

L • W
A
token
of love

E P

ABCDEFGHI
JKLMNOPQ
RSTUVW
XYZ
abcdefghijklmno
pqrstuvwxyz
1234567890
ABCDEFGHIJKL
MNOPQRSTUV
WXYZ

PROJECTS

The collection of Quaker motifs began in the late eighteenth century. The motifs remained in sampler form and were never used for embellishments on everyday items. However, with the popularity of Quaker motifs today, the patterns can be adapted to adorn many items: pincushions, pillows, book covers, cards, anniversary pictures, frames, bags, purses, clothes and of course your own sampler designs.

In this section I give you a couple of project ideas to get you started.

A S
T C
20 22
L M
L K

L D
S J
FRIENDSHIP
MY
TOKEN
OF LOVE

PROJECT 1:
QUAKER MOTIF HEART

There are a variety of Quaker patterns on both sides of the heart. It can be used to celebrate weddings, engagements, anniversaries, the birth of a new baby or other happy events. The open emblem is ideal for including initials if you want to personalize your heart, and the empty area around the emblem can include dates. There is an alphabet and numbers graph so that you can copy letters and numbers onto the main design if you wish (see page 125).

Making up instructions

1. Complete the two designs from charts A and B on pages 124–125 and cut around the border line, leaving 5mm (¼in) spare around the edge.

2. Fold the edge over along the stitch line, all the way round.

3. With a sharp needle and one strand of thread, position the two halves wrong sides together, matching the stitch line. Catch only the stitch not the fabric and overstitch every stitch.

4. Continue until you reach the top centre of the heart and insert the ribbon, fold in half and position the loose ends inside the heart. Continue sewing, catching the ribbon at the centre point to make it secure. Continue overstitching until there is a 6cm (2⅜in) gap left.

5. Insert the soft wadding/batting evenly into the heart, making sure all corner areas are filled. Using a knitting needle to push the wadding in gently will help.

6. When you are happy with the amount of wadding/batting in the heart, continue to overstitch and close up the edge.

Size

12.5 x 11cm (5 x 4¼in)

Materials

Fabric

16ct aida or 32ct evenweave, 42 x 28cm (16½ x 11in)

DMC stranded cotton

2 skeins of red mix 4210

Tapestry needle

Size 24

Ribbon

Cream or red, 21cm (8¼in) long and 5mm (¼in) wide

Soft wadding/batting

Sharp embroidery scissors

Knitting needle

A

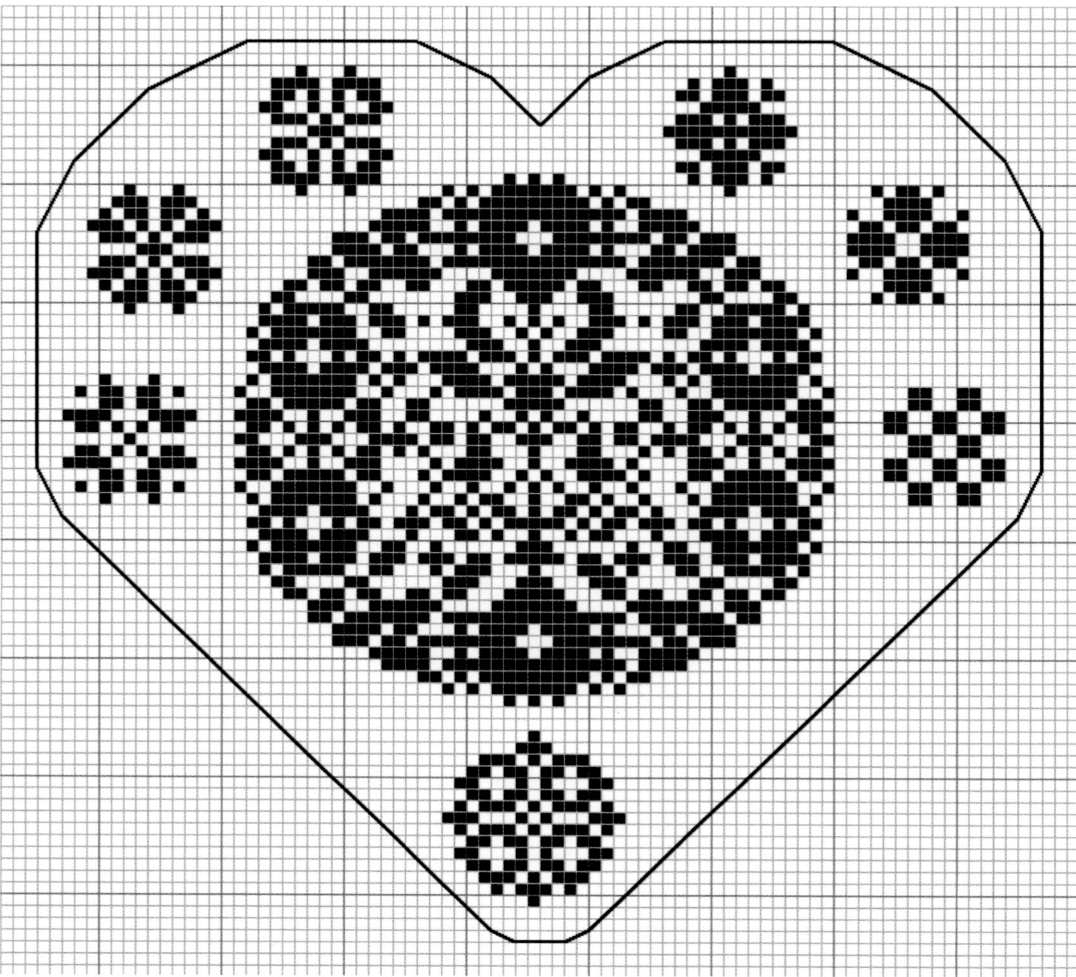

Key

Cross stitch

Back stitch

B

ABCDEFGHI
JKLMNOPQR
STUVWXYZ
1234567890

PROJECT 2:
PINCUSHION

The half medallion patterns can be made into circles by mirroring the pattern. This square is made into a pincushion, but can be made into a wedding keepsake to celebrate the date, or a wedding ring holder by attaching a ribbon in the centre. It would make an ideal gift on a special day such as an anniversary, birth or graduation by adding initials and dates. Use the alphabet and numbers graph on page 125 to copy letters and numbers onto the main design.

Making up instructions

1. Complete the design from chart A on page 128 and trim around the outside of the back stitch line, leaving 1cm (⅜in) extra.

2. Fold over the fabric along the back stitching.

3. Complete the back stitched square from chart B. Place pieces A and B wrong sides together. Hold both back stitch edges next to each other and attach with slip stitch along all four sides of the square.

4. On the fourth edge of the square leave a 5cm (2in) gap for stuffing the pouch with wadding/batting. Use a knitting needle to make sure that it reaches the inside corners. When there is enough wadding/batting, continue to slip stitch to the end and secure the thread.

Size

71 x 73 stitch count

9 x 9cm (3½ x 3½in)

Materials

Fabric

18ct aida, 20 x 30cm (8 x 11¾in)

Using alternative fabric may affect the finished size

DMC stranded cotton

1 skein of blue/pink mix 4215

Use 2 threads throughout

Tapestry needle

Size 24

Soft wadding/batting

Sharp embroidery scissors

Knitting needle

A

Key

- Cross stitch
- Back stitch

B